OPHELIA ON ACID

POEMS

JENNIFER BRADPIECE

༄

BLUE HORSE PRESS REDONDO BEACH, CALIFORNIA 2021

OPHELIA ON ACID

JENNIFER BRADPIECE

Blue Horse Press
Redondo Beach,
California

Copyright © 2021 by Jennifer Bradpiece
All rights reserved
Printed in the United States of America

Cover art: "Queen of the Night"
by Heather Anne Welch ©
Used by permission

Editors: Jeffrey and Tobi Alfier
Blue Horse Press logo: Amy Lynn Alfier (1996)

ISBN 978-0-578-69098-8

No part of this book may be reproduced or transmitted in any form or by any means, electronic or mechanical, including photocopy, recording, or any information storage and retrieval system now known or to be invented, without permission in writing from the publisher, except by a reviewer who wishes to quote brief passages in connection with a review written for inclusion in a magazine, newspaper or broadcast.

FIRST EDITION © 2021

This and other Blue Horse Press Titles may be found at www.bluehorsepress.com

In remembrance of Cat and Heather

Acknowledgments

Gratitude to the following journals for publishing, or accepting for future publication, poems from this manuscript:

Anti-Heroin Chic: "Coffee Grounds," "Smiles of my Dead," and "What We're Left With Sometimes," *The Chickasaw Plum Review*: "Time," *The Common Ground Review*: "The Archivists," *Cultural* Weekly: "The Humans" (published as "Lullaby for a Species"); *Black Napkin Press*: "Before the Fall," *Breath and Shadow*: "You Ask me Why I Wear Bright Colors," *Edgar Allen Poets*: "A Place Called Well," *Ekphrastic Review*: "How to Paint Pain," *Mas Tequila Review*: "Holding On," *Media Cake*: "In Praise of Funny Socks" and "Real," *Memory House Magazine*: "I Find You," *The Nervous Breakdown*: "Overgrown," *Nowhere Poetry*: "Meeting Herself at 35" (published as "What Meeting Herself at 35 was Like"), *Our Loss Anthology*: "Daybook of the Dead," *The Pagan Muse Anthology*: "Consorting with Ereshkigal," *Paper Nautilus*: "Thirteenth Floor," *Poetic Diversity*: "Beetle" and "Half the Story," *Please See Me*: "Self by Prescription" and "Thin Hair," *Quaint Magazine*: "The Broken Bone," *Redactions*: "Chronic V Terminal," *Requiem Magazine*: "Techno-Dreams," *Rip Rap Journal*: "Biography," *San Pedro River Review*: "Re-animation Aubade," *Stimulus—Respond*: "Life Lines" and "The Release" (published as "Through Time"), *Whiskey Fish Review*: "The Day the Answers Fled," *Wicked Banshee Press*:" Urge to Make Things Ugly.

Contents

Preface: Pansies, That's for Thoughts…

15   Ophélie by Arthur Rimbaud

ACTS

I To Be…

19   How to Paint Pain
21   One through Ten
23   Self by Prescription
25   Pain Cycle
27   Shut-In
29   Tango
30   Thin Hair
32   You Ask Me Why I Wear Bright Colors
33   The Broken Bone
34   Re-animation Aubade
36   Waking up Broken Again
38   Some Needles
39 – 41   How You Are parts I & II

II Or Not…

45   The Urge to Make Things Ugly
46   A Place Called "Well"
49   Offerings
50   Consorting with Ereshkigal
51   Meeting Herself at 35
53   Techno-Dreams
55   Overgrown

56 In Praise of Funny Socks
57 Sometimes
59 Real
60 Beetle
61 Before the Fall
63 The Day the Answers Fled
65 The Thing Is
69 Holding On
71 Thirteenth Floor

III Rosemary, That's for Remembrance...

75 The Archivists
77 Daybook of the Dead
79 Time
80 I Find You
81 Twenty Year Age Difference
83 Biography
86 Life Lines
87 The Release
90 Half the Story
92 Do You?
93 Coffee Grounds
95 Smiles of my Dead
97 The Humans
99 What We're Left with Sometimes
100 Chronic vs Terminal

CODA Reflections

104 Untitled # 1 by Heather Anne Welch (2013)
105 Untitled # 2 by Jennifer Bradpiece (2019)
About the Author

Preface: Pansies, That's for Thoughts…

*As well as symbolizing thoughts and love, pansies are also said to represent sympathizing with an other's pain, suffering, and distress.

We are all underwater. Gracefully jellyfishing. Pummeled against riverbeds. All, occasionally, drowning. We swim against stream. We float. At times we desperately cry out in the crush of the river's frenzied rush. Grotesquely or subtly, we attempt to tread the hungry waters so we can hold others in their fall. We are, all of us, fish-eye lensed and gasping for others to see us in our struggle and swell. Sometimes, when others see us, we dissolve.

Ophelia is a character that captures and haunts our imagination. Even if only in a symbolic way. If we stare at her too long, she evaporates. While her lines are few and her character mostly meek in Shakespeare's *Hamlet*, there are far more interesting qualities and metaphors attributed to her in modern poems, music, and fiction. Particularly when she is rewritten by women. Perhaps exactly the same qualities that diminish in her original walk across the stage and float down the river, in some other light, are illuminated, "with a difference." That she is a touch "seer," a purely relational being, an entirely referential and metaphorical character, for instance. Or that she inhabits the liminal spaces of madness, water, and death.

Maybe there's an Ophelia who finds another world underwater…

I often don't know where I stand apart from relational interpersonal or inter-meshed intimacies. With others, with writing or art, or with psychedelic plants and substances. Cited always in webs of metaphor, I locate myself more in co-collaboration as connective tissue and quick transmuting simile than in declaration. Unlike Ophelia, I have rarely needed to be connected to a specific other in a definitive way. Yet, the need to connect through nonlinear means in a linear world combined with seeing the invisible currents that shape that world—a world which seems often to have taken a vow of blindness against multiplicity—can feel equally tragic.

We walk by metaphorical rivers each day, not recognizing water as mirror or portal. Pain, aging, and dying are ineffable spaces that often defy language. Ophelia is a character who embodies these liminal spaces, and, perhaps because of this, has little voice.

As with many artists and porous beings, my ability to bear and carry the world ebbs and flows ferociously. My reference points with others are tenuous in the best of circumstances. My interior life and connection to the world is lush but hard to translate. This is how I entered my near life-long relationship with chronic illness and pain.

I've been diagnosed with ME/CFS and Fibromyalgia for well over two decades. These illnesses affect every system from skin to gut. My IBS often acts as if it were Crohn's. I suffer chronic intractable migraines (both ocular and vestibular) with intense neck involvement. There are bouts of acute vertigo, and near constant low to high grade motion sickness and ear pain and pressure issues. Degenerative discs and stenosis in my spine and neck flared to a near constant roaring a couple years after a hip replacement. With the addition of years, structural pain worsens, and new health conditions arise, like adult asthma. The flares triggered by weather change and sensitivities to air on an ailing planet ratchet everything up.

To be in pain and ill all the time. Everything makes you sick. You feel so fragile in this world among others, especially as you age. These invisible yet constant experiences shape your life and relationships at every level. While grateful, you feel in turns a burden to and perversely resentful of loved ones who are caretakers (if you are lucky enough to have them). Being left behind by your peers in an ever- widening gap. Often being unbelieved, misread, or having your reality denied or met with silence. To be so often dismissed by those in the medical profession. To be looked at by stranger, family, and friend as crazy, lazy, or addict. These outside voices and attitudes will drown you faster than the rushing of your shrinking days. Not because your worth hinges on what others think of you, but because you are faced with the evidence you are not enough and you should be doing more by your every brush with the external workings of the world. At some point, it may feel even our fierce creativity fails us. And we slowly lose a common world connected to shared experiences with the able-bodied people in our lives —this is its own form of madness.

For those of us who live with invisible chronic illness, these realities put in question our own relationship with sanity as we cultivate a grueling and premature familiarity with the realities of advanced age and the specter of death. If we are lucky, some one or few people will catch us. If we are lucky, and luck has a big role in being caught by any system we live within, we might create and expand our internal horizons.

I am not alone in the belief that people's inability or unwillingness to attempt to understand invisible chronic illness from the inside out has much to do with our Western culture's fear around the unknown. Our society's terror when confronted by aging, the process of dying, and death. Death and madness as tragic or romantic metaphor in poetry, music, prose, and visual art are well mapped. Yet, dealing with these subjects unflinchingly and head on has the potential to make an audience especially uncomfortable. In life and in art.

For years, I publicly shared mostly the magic of seeing differently. My strange eyesight from amblyopia since childhood. My alien anthropologist's stance. I emphasized how pain and illness force creativity. At some point your illness is less deniable in every moment–less disposed to being medicated-down for brief adventures or to be hidden away until you can deal with full shutdowns when you are alone—that aftermath which can go on and on for days and days. Expressing *around* and not *through* your daily reality, trying to share only the beauty, depletes your ability to be seen and ask for help. Once these conditions integrate into the entirety of your every waking moment, it may be too late.

I had done what many do and held to myself the impossible of my survival for so long, when it got decades worse, I began to render my whole being invisible. And there will be a time for many Painlings (as my friend Cat called us) when there must be room for the stark realities of our moment-to-moment survival. An access intimacy between our loved ones. Space to speak and be heard and not feel like you are just a complaining energy drag. Like a sudden turn in the river, you find yourself screaming *see me* and, more importantly, *see the many like me*. If we are met with silence or ridicule, further self-isolation often feels like the only refuge.

Anne Sexton wrote, "Live or die, but don't poison everything." For many of us, as it was in the end for her, this paradigm feels unattainable. Navigating through our days often feels like treading water while hooked to an IV of noxious poison. We try to contain the venom, yet inevitably, some escapes. When our very neurology is constantly attacking us, we are often trapped in fight or flight. This cycle of fear and darkness can build and turn us against ourselves and those we love most. Living with chronic illness and pain often attunes us to the world in intense and specific ways. Like Ophelia, we beckon from the deep waters we have found or are forced to inhabit. When we reach out, we feel invisible. For many this leads to retreat. Some, like Ophelia, take their own lives. Whether from sheer exhaustion, insufficient medical support, or lack of being seen, suicide is unsurprisingly the leading cause of death in the chronic pain / invisibly ill community. Through this liquid figure in Shakespeare's existential *Hamlet*, I hope to open a space for recognition and conversation. A space for understanding each passing moment's survival in a chronically ill body as an art. A space beyond the ambitious frenzied existence of our current time. A liminal space between.

Jennifer Bradpiece

Ophélie by Arthur Rimbaud

~ translated by Oliver Bernard: Arthur Rimbaud,
Collected Poems (1962)

I

On the calm black water where the stars are sleeping
White Ophelia floats like a great lily;
Floats very slowly, lying in her long veils...
- In the far-off woods you can hear them sound the mort.

For more than a thousand years sad Ophelia
Has passed, a white phantom, down the long black river.
For more than a thousand years her sweet madness
Has murmured its ballad to the evening breeze.

The wind kisses her breasts and unfolds in a wreath
Her great veils rising and falling with the waters;
The shivering willows weep on her shoulder,
The rushes lean over her wide, dreaming brow.

The ruffled water-lilies are sighing around her;
At times she rouses, in a slumbering alder,
Some nest from which escapes a small rustle of wings;
- A mysterious anthem falls from the golden stars.

II

O pale Ophelia! beautiful as snow!
Yes child, you died, carried off by a river!
- It was the winds descending from the great mountains of Norway
That spoke to you in low voices of better freedom.

It was a breath of wind, that, twisting your great hair,
Brought strange rumors to your dreaming mind;
It was your heart listening to the song of Nature
In the groans of the tree and the sighs of the nights;

It was the voice of mad seas, the great roar,
That shattered your child's heart, too human and too soft;
It was a handsome pale knight, a poor madman
Who one April morning sate mute at your knees!

I
To Be....

"I've always walked the ragged edge."

~Lisa Mantchev, *Eyes Like Stars*

How to Paint Pain

Canvas must be skin.
A hide pulled tight.
Gesso the canvas by allowing
a gossamer stream of saliva to fall
onto your palm. Rub into skin.
Like a balm softening the hide.
Now split yourself open.
Use a scalpel to find the fissure
where muscles and tendons open.
Stretch one across for texture.
Snap off the radius where it meets the ulna.
Dip the heart shaped end to
the pool inside your elbow.
Hold it over your head like a half note.
Wave long and short strokes onto the
canvas. Circle your abdomen
until the skin swirls open exposing
the coiled intestinal maze.
For a balance of earth tones:
Take what is left in the bowels
with both palms. Carve yourself
open to the clavicle. Break off
the smallest rib for finer detail.
Open your lungs to lacquer over the clotting.
Plunge a fingernail into your inner ear.
Now blow to heat what lingers there.
Use this encaustic to seal the layers.
Now you may sign your work

by pressing the veins
of your heart against its corner.
If you've created something you
could live with daily on your wall,
begin again.

One Through Ten

Doctor,

Your question,
my chronic pain.
My answer,
at your request, 1-10.

But first, tell me
1-10: how much you love
each of your children?

1-10: how much you would miss your sibling
versus your spouse?

1-10: how you would order
your senses?
Lose the wild raspberry and amber
spray of sunset, versus
the scent of your newborn's skin?

1-10: where your passions fall?
Your successes, your failures,
your dreams?

I am not sure, at all, Doctor,
you understand the weight
1-10 implicates—the hidden
balances, agendas, the compensatory scales.

If I were to tell you
that the way down is deep,
the sinking long,
and you won't make the next narrow pass
without two oars,
Doctor, which *one* would you choose?

Self by Prescription

O, the oblong, kidney-shaped,
apricot-serrated, pillow-round,
pale blue dream—

There is a science in balancing
the pills' volatile contradictory calendars,
alkalizing conflicting agendas.

This one unearths
ice picks from ocular nerve,
ear drum, and dims thoughts'
evasive aura. My senses
pulsate into floor boards.

That one puppets
marionette limbs
to lift plate to sink.
Jell-O'd muscles give,
as water washes plate
straight through hands.
A porcelain symphony scrapes
across metal sink sides,
and shatters my skull.

And this one controls pain's
acute expiration date;
forecloses the hollow
bone house left
when the nuclear glow gives way;
allows me to swallow the dull throb,
the nauseous air, the heady light.

The death knell for my
natural senses sounded
over two decades ago.

Un-medicated cells,
that fluidly carried
the organs' rhythms and
the flesh's thesaurus,
are a lost country.
Each line on that
globe leading back
has been undone by
chalky erasers.

My skin's ship docked
far from any known
topography or ancient
map's lost sea.

There is an art
to pouring yourself
out of so many bottles.

I am mixing up a new galaxy.
I am naming every star
some piece of me.

Pain Cycle

Fingertips
see more sometimes,
each swirling print like an iris.

Pupils in take light,
while fingers gauge weight,
assess temperature,
measure pores
by their inversion
or conversion.

Day imprints its hours
beneath the skin,
in tightened ligaments,
knots of memory that strangle
circulation.

Heel of the hand recirculates
regret into forgiveness,
redirects the alchemy
of what we keep,
what we let go.

Breath, an oxygen tsunami,
resurrects red in sallow cheeks.
Blood blooms sensation
into numb limbs.

The fingers, the palm, the heel,
the side of the hand is God
against the mountain ridge
between shoulder and spine;

reminders that redemption
is every day on this earth
as transfusion
through the flesh and bones
of an other.

Shut-In

"This is a confused and frightened world,
but it's a world to run away from"
~sample from beginning of Funki Porcini's track "Back Home"

The mirrors
get confusing, and
quite often
the compass breaks.

There is a constant
metronome:
the swallows, the crickets,
the settling house,
every clock.

Do I own a clock that ticks?

There is a tendency to walk
in circles,
to be unaware of
how often
we talk to ourselves.
One reason
we have cats.

There is often
an issue with scale
or perspective—
how to measure one's
movements in the space of time
with little back drop
and no greater current to
swim against.

The weight of things
becomes immeasurable—
a problem of ballast.
Are you sinking into the floor
or floating up towards the ceiling?

There is a trap
in forgetting how to love
and getting lost.
Or is it a trap of forgetting
how to wish
to be found?

In any case.
It's not all confusion.

The shutting in
allows great relief
in all it is possible
to shut out.

Tango

When pain is constant
you are variable.
What you love,
subtracted and
sieved away.

When pain is constant
the world is conditional.
When not impossible.
A sharp-toothed abacus bead
cuts heart-wires
shreds through you.

When pain is constant
floors are slippery.
Nerves dance in
shadowed corners
of crowded rooms.
Your passions spin,
dip you from view.

Thin Hair

Each Botox doctor praises my thin hair.
At least seven times, during the migraine quelling
thirty shots to the skull and neck,
they comment encouragingly on
my *"nice thin hair."*
How they "find the spots *so* easily"
with their impressive needles full of Botulism.

"Oh, see how easy it is with your *nice thin hair?*"
they comment repeatedly, without a hint of irony.
My head blushes. My split ends preen.

I am used to needles loving my "*big green veins.*"
But my meager locks have never commanded such praise.
I imagine the doctors despairing over a thick mane,
tsking as they worry through the brush of a more populated head.
They say "thick hair" as if they might murmur "tough luck."

The beauty standards have been reversed,
and I imagine now, on the outside, strip malls filled
with hair-thinning salons, sashed with huge banners
declaring: "rid yourself of unwanted extra hairs on your head
—half price—grand opening!"

Ads pop up on news feeds everywhere:
"Tired of looking like you are about to appear in shampoo
commercials? Banish unsightly fullness from your scalp:
30 day money back guarantee!"

On my way out of the office, I note the young woman
going in after me. Her hair, a black lagoon at midnight,
an ink well spilt over onyx. A pang of pity stabs my temple.
I turn and whisper, "don't take it too hard."

You Ask Me Why I Wear Bright Colors

Pain is vivid -
the vibrant teal and fuchsia of veins.
The crimson gush of persimmon
down the chin or forearm, the golden puss
as a scab bubbles the skin inside out,
the snap of bone that scintillates
in kaleidoscopic fractals behind the eyes,
throbbing bruises of tangerine and periwinkle
as skull-bone or knee-joint knocks
into shelf edge or desk leg.
The plum kiss left behind on elbow
or hip-bone.

When the vibrant colors dissolve,
dimness reigns-
the faded blues of ice packs,
taupe heating pad covers,
dull crimping aches that cloud mind, fog motion.
The skin is a pin cushion for metallic gray
needles delivering clear cortisone elixirs.
Amber prescription bottles, the muted pills:
pillows of white, pale blue, butter yellow;
the oblong, the round, the capsule.

Now, place your head to my chest
and listen: the sound inside
is the peacock's cry—strangled.

The Broken Bone

Years grind against the axis of bone,
continents drifting in marrow waters
eroding their topography in time.

My eleventh year a horse threw me like a shoe:
unlaced me where pleasure would hinge.
The broken bone grew into a bad fist.
It will clench cold while I am wrapped around a lover.
It will stab into its crescent socket
as I hurry downstairs.
My youth will buckle here.

This phantom femur radiates lost rhythms:
where dancing began, where dancing will seize.
A swivel will reveal the vulnerable bend,
and the world will stiffen.

It is right. The hips being
the inevitable site
of tectonic shift in woman.

Re-animation Aubade

Sunlight: the metal edge
of a paint stripping knife
tearing a fissure between my skin
and the black tar octaves
of the night's oblivion.

'Morning, anvil, 'morning, ice pick,
prescription-filmed tongue, frosted bones, mummy limbs,
good morning, morning after.

I am pre-re-animation, as the fingernails
of dark limp limbo still scrape against my back.
I don't know whose bones flatten the bed,
whose nerves twitch like strobes, whose
skin I'm waking up in.

A steady hand reaches for me
from the dawn drenched shadows.
And somewhere inside the pitch,
I know your voice.

My numb hand begins to register
its place in yours. Slowly, you work up
the bones of my hand with your
fingertips and palms.

Reconstruct me.
Build me up from the twisted
pillows and haul me out
the grotesque halls of dream.
Roll out my shoulder muscles.
Carefully pack me in ice,
a frozen Persephone,
guiding the ship of my exanimate
vessel back to land.

So faithfully I set stones in place to
crumble me the night before:
each pill doll, each bourbon sip,
each hash hit, like buoys that
ferry me across my temporary River Styx.

Without an usher I would certainly
drift there, in permanent transition,
just off the brightening shore.

Good morning, long hard swallow
into sand.

Waking up Broken Again

The mornings you wake up
accident victim.
Ballard crash.
Did someone "get off?"
You hope so.

Or maybe you wake from
the mad finale
of a spy movie they
make over and over.
Or it was the FBI?
You were thrown from a building.
You shouldn't have survived.

Your partner smiles at you
and a rage storms.
It's not the face
but the smile.
The incongruence of a misplaced
line that fails to figure.

You must be in a hospital.
They forgot to turn on the drip.
Are you in traction?
Post-surgery?
Your knees have been taken out.
Your neck and back must be broken.

Later the smile will kindly
offer breakfast.
Confusing you.
Isn't your jaw wired shut?

Light shimmers through
the bedroom window.
You only feel the ice packs
on your head and neck.

The birds sound like car alarms.

It will happen again tomorrow.

Some Needles

are knives
quick cutting
to bowed sorrows,
sewing dreams to the hem
of your skin.

Healing is adhesion
after a letting.
Nebulous galaxies
surface and bloom.
Explode and scatter.
Cluster and reabsorb.

The more complete,
the more brutal
the fusion.

How You Are ~ Part I

When people ask
and you speak of
your pain and your sick,
even a little,
you can see their eyes glaze over
and something shrink back.
As if you were talking about death.
And, around the edges, you are.

Some refer to their pain
as if it were their identity.
Illustrating, quite suddenly,
to all in a room
how we can drown
in identity.

But some of us
attempt to hand over
a tiny fragile looking-glass
to see through.
To locate where we are
attempting to emerge from.
So, if we make little sense
or forget our nouns and dates
or shatter a glass
or seem distracted and sharp edged,
there's a baseline of grace.

We are trying to give that grace
to ourselves and often failing.
So we know how hard it is.
Especially in the abstract.

And pain, like death,
is always abstract.
Until it's not.

How you Are ~Part II

When death hangs
thick around
for several years,
in the concrete ephemeral,
it is hard for many to remember
they are still part of the living.
But when your body is sick and wracked,
the liminal space between
is blurred
by a moment to moment
reminder
multiplied by the air
subtracted by your breath,
and you,
your life now,
is a strange
remainder.

II

Or Not....

"Suicide is, after all, the opposite of the poem."

~Anne Sexton

The Urge to Make Things Ugly

Slices shards of amber glass through fleshy toes in sparkling sand
Pries the legs off fuzzy green caterpillars
Scrapes a chiffon scarf down the peeling paint of an alley wall
Drives rusty nails into polished rosewood
Loosens salt caps on immaculately set tables
Scuffs tarry streaks across a freshly mopped floor
Clamps teeth tightly around tin foil
Knows you know exactly how it feels
Shatters the crystal vase of roses against a vanity mirror
Bites a manicured cuticle until the hangnail bleeds
Smears lipstick the color of clotted blood
Claws silk stockings over long pale thighs
Jams a new stiletto heel against the concrete floor
Spills red wine across white linens
Teeters over to the three-legged desk
Perches on an empty corner
Never gets invited back

A Place Called Well

Now they wish to introduce me
to a place called Well.
Can one reach an appropriate destination
by swimming in the sand with boots on?

I see my way to Well through
someone else's window.
Well refuses my imagination,
will not be tried on the way
fantasy might a prospective lover.

Well waits on the shelf of some dried goods store
all chewy brown and wrinkled sweet.

Well floats by my left thigh
like some slippery silvered fish.

Well mocks me with its steady job.

Well marries in a white dress and
bears three smiling children.

Well rolls around like a glass eye that
watches me but doesn't care.

Well lines tiny shoes in two straight rows,
starches laundry, washes faces,
feeds the dog, packs school lunches,
throws birthday parties and cocktail parties
and never drinks too much wine.

Well produces home movies of family trips,
wraps presents for under the Christmas tree,
cooks breakfasts and dinners
and never burns the roast.

Well gets wrinkled from meetings with teachers
and greeting the guests.

Well rests contented in the afternoon,
cries old blue tears at borrowed weddings.

Well sighs, smug in the evening,
boasts photographs of grandchildren.

Well haunts me like an hourglass
on the mantle, running out of time.

And how will I know Well?

I don't even know enough
to ease down in its rocking chair
wearing down the floorboards.

Well sits in the sitting room.
I dance on the rooftop,
dangle from a telephone wire.

Offerings

The logic of taking care
of a body
turned against itself
plays hide-and-seek
for years.

Strengthen aching muscles.
Increase the exhausted pulse.
Soak and massage tender skin
that slinks from touch.
Fill the fickle gut with grains
and fruit as if a holy thing.
Press paper offerings
through unforgiving bones.
Worship the burning altar,
tiny votive in trembling hands.

Release the senses from
their enamel vault.
Blur of vision, sting of scent,
incense wafting, alive
through jagged glass windows.
A letting, the only
reasonable worship.

Consorting with Ereshkigal

Inanna, Heaven's Queen,
hangs from a meat hook.
She dangles in her sister's realm;
dripping flesh from bone
in willing surrender—
to be stripped away,
to be reborn.

At the fire, the women dance,
together they sing.
They remember their dark sister,
revel in Her wild process.
They reacquaint themselves with
what they knew.
They enter
to be stripped away,
to be reborn.

At her desk, a woman cries and
stares out the window.
Her doctor suggests Prozac.
Her sister prescribes a day at the spa.
Her boyfriend diagnoses "hysteria."
All of them whisper,
quick to name her.

She is consorting with Ereshkigal.
She is a goddess
hanging on a meat hook.

Meeting Herself at 35

She sat beside herself attentively
for so long,
she had to be reintroduced —
forgot how to form words,
lips tight as waxed rope,
filmy as seaweed,
puffy as chrysanthemums.
Forgot how to listen,
cauliflower ear packed
with dandelion petals,
no wind for wishes between
walls, between eucalyptus trees,
bark soft as skin.
Kept snuffing out the cigarette
she'd just lit, a tiny amber
ember volleyed back and forth
between darkness and thumb
pressed fire. Unlooped her own
knitting as if each wound and tightened
thread was a stitch of a shroud
against each blinking neon
green minute on the digital clock,
keeping time, keeping time,
not as the ¾ time of a minuet
or a counting of the tabla,
or the way a kitten winds
the pink yarn across a room, but holding
it, as a taupe teddy bear in a closed closet,
or the bone-beaded hand of her mother
as she passed over.
She argued the same point endlessly,

countering unintended opinions etched
in the rectangles of public bathroom stalls.
She invented new bombs, while contemplating
peace, pulled on every eyelash she'd
just curled, discovered new diseases with
each dreamt vaccine, while the raindrops
divided on the roof and windows like cells under
a fingernail-thin glass slide — the microscope
lens of the moon, the only named thing
that separated her from sky.

Techno-Dreams

One thousand things passed under my window,
all of them deadly.

The parade of corpses,
every one of them without feet.
I was grateful that they passed almost in silence.

There was a carousel of centaurs:
part man, part machine.
I thought I recognized the faces,
but they passed me blindly, every one.

Ice skaters slid by like radio waves
with featureless faces and nonsense mouths.
I tried to echo them, but my lips couldn't form the words.

Dogs with metal tongues growled on the street
swallowing mailboxes whole.
Delivery men chased them
with remote controls screaming, "Malfunction!"

There was text transposed in the air.
I had to read the lines vertically,
upset because I couldn't lie down.

White coats with huge eyes and no ears
climbed through my window,
renamed my organs and rearranged my bones.
I found my fingers attached to my neck:
had to write in a blind backbend.

My snooze bar became
a delete button.
I pressed it, and everything
reappeared.

Overgrown

Something flees inside you. Rises
a trail of ashes into smoke.
You wonder with the low hum of the microwave,
melting ice off cocooned yellow carrots,
if radiation burrows beneath skin
like hairless rabbits, if the mobile
phone speaks on a cellular level,
how the toxic pacification of a cigarette
singes a life line.
Outside, the screams from city streets
remind you that survival is
as possible as instant soup
without sanity's gourmet trappings.
Honking horns and sirens warn
of near misses and sudden deaths.
The day swings, the hours shift like
a large lady on a park bench trading gravity
from one thigh to the other.
Silence comes to somebody in trash bag bedding.
You slip a peach pill between pink lips
and imagine the silk-lined reception
of black sky, stars scattered like playthings—
shiny, plastic, hollow—
slinking coils, spinning tops, wall-eyed marbles,
concentric circles rippling in platitude and epitaph,
the word residue inside a coffin night.
Here the darkness speaks in code, shoots around
and between language and silence, echoing
in sleep's caverns, wafting, tangling,
unkempt desires grown over stone.

In Praise of Funny Socks

Nobody ever dies in funny socks.
Sure, a clown somewhere,
clobbered by a giant rubber daisy
came to his end
in red floppy oversized shoes.

Funny socks are a safety measure,
I told myself,
on amphetamine-amped nights
alone in the dark,
hugging pillow to chest,
heart pounding through the bedsprings.

Perhaps tomorrow
the last-breath-tango
in sparkling stilettos,
lips red and wet as a fresh wound.
But not a solo trembling footnote-death.
So I'd stretch icy feet into the
funniest socks I could find.

Still, some nights,
walking alone on city streets,
perceiving sinister footsteps behind me
my heart pounding into purse straps,
I imagine my feet striding in
fuzzy rainbow toe-sock steps
and somehow feel safe.

Sometimes

Our shared lips
and your petal fingers
sometimes pale
to the comfort I kept
in my palm.
The death I breathe
to unpoison myself
and allow
the world to enter
on my terms.
The kindest light
is powder soft.
It burns through my senses —
an execution's charred remains.
Counting away nightmares,
division with a razor blade.
Sniffing the thorns of roses,
their redness bubbles
down my chin,
stains kisses on the mirror —
the window where
I see myself
whenever I look in.
All the lights
thrown on at once
for one brief
brilliant season.

Before it buries me,
I must escape
this toxic Eden.
Although,
at the time
it feels as innocent
as dancing in the snow
as a little girl
at grandpa's house
two days before
Christmas.

Real

You write...
Perhaps you like to think you start with wood.
Perhaps you start with wood and then you chisel the eyes,
wide enough for detail, but narrow cornered,
so as not to take in too much light.
Then a nose, for specific scents only.
Two secret lips that might speak.
You want the wood to live and breath; you want it real.

Perhaps you think the magic dust that makes it real is vodka or
cocaine. Maybe you think it's speed or Xanax or sex with
strangers. Or maybe it's the cigarettes or the angle the light hits
the wall across from you.

And maybe it is sex with strangers.
But maybe it is sex with yourself.
Maybe the poem is sex and you are the stranger.
Maybe the poem is stranger than you.
Maybe the poem *is* real.
Maybe the poem is more real than the event it recalls.
Maybe the event the poem is based on only feels real
on the page, as a poem.

Maybe that's when you realize that your life is the wood
and you and your psychiatrist
have very different ideas
about what makes wood real.

Beetle

splits its body in half
bounces across the ceiling
tries to mate with its shadow
strikes its echo
over and over

plastic wing waltz
taps out codes of desire
not so unlike us
lonely wings torn
hidden

Before the Fall

To have known you before
the capillaries burst
and the veins strained
beneath our skins.
Before the lights
of cities burned
out, atomic, before our eyes.
Before pupils grew
and widened
to accommodate every
misplaced thing.
Before the lining
of our coats tore
and our fingers
sifted what sieved away
too late.
Before the needles
pierced the marrow.
Before the prepositions
took over.
Before the hearts
clapped shut like
chimney flues.
Before our feet wore
grooves in silence.

Before the bones
shattered in their sockets.
Before pencil lead
snapped and cindered.
Before our checkbooks
balanced zero.
Before the skies
swept the calendar clean.

The Day the Answers Fled

the house moved away
with its white halls
and uneasy storage.
Folded up each box
of a room.
Blew the echo out
the fireplace,
the frozen faces
off the mantle,
the vacuum
packed air.
Shook out the yard
and covered
the nostalgia
in linens.
Each bedroom burst
like overfilled balloons
leaving only spent dreams
on the skeleton of a bookcase.
The tea kettle
whistled once
and the whole kitchen
rattled. Utensils
and chopstick exclamations
clamored, and the bricks
dismantled each memory carefully.
The garage: shovel, trowel, and iron
dug and smoothed
the secrets out to seed the lawn.
Twisted trees bared rotting fruit

for years, each fleshed with one
eye pressed tightly shut.
The neighbors all had
conflicting stories
and scratched their heads
around the bicycles and leashed dogs.
Only fragments of foundation
remained in the shape
of a question mark.
The questions mounted
the forgotten bookcase
until it collapsed.
The address numbers
spelled an epitaph:
Home is assembled
only at the site
of violent deconstruction.

The Thing Is

"In a dream you are never eighty" ~ Anne Sexton

I've written half
the lines below
a thousand times
over the last decade.

Written and
scratched out
the other half
as many times or more.

The truth is
for longer than it did not,
every invite carries
the ominous weight
of a jury summons.

And every adventure
we've shared
signals in my nerves
as much stress
as excitement.

The thing is
I've always been
near equal parts
terrified of
and intoxicated by
this world.

And, now every day
I don't go out,
something else settles in:

a pleasure in the pain of it.
That cuticle bleed.
The toothpick pushed too deep.
And I have no idea
how to proceed
when I must go.
So it is always
a must go.

The truth is, the thing is
I often close my eyes
and run my finger
along your names
in my phone,
remembering what
you smell like
(unless you wear
too much perfume).

The thing is, the truth is
I'm often eighty in a
forty year old body.
(Doctors say:
"Well, you won't
feel any worse
when you're eighty.")

The truth is
each year, I do—
each year, a something new.
So I know the bait
moves up ahead.
An exhaustion accumulates
filling in the breathy gaps.

The thing is
for years now,
my birthday wish
has been the courage
to ask you to feel
my love there, even
when I'm not.

The truth is
I could almost abandon
these few cigarettes
each day, but have
no measures left
for counting time.

My hours pass on an
abacus in flames.
Each color turns to ash,
and I know the game
of solitaire
is nearly won
until tomorrow.

The thing is
I vacillate
between asking you
to leave me be
and begging you
to be my lure—
to snap at the end of the line.
To quicken the decoy.
To make it jump and shimmer
with an immediacy
I can't ignore.

The thing is, these truths
are simultaneous.
Address all letters to:
The Tension Between.
But not too many at once.
But don't stop writing.
But write it all in glitter glue
so the message sticks
and my greyhound heart
forgets its cage
and runs.

Holding On

Press 2 to speak to no one in Spanish.

Press 3 if you are thrilled by endless repetition.

Your call is very important to us, the electronic pantheon above, the faithful will be rewarded, please continue to hold.

Press 4 if you are tuned to a one-way radio wave.

Press 5 if you are beginning to believe that Earth is as flat as your keypad.

We are experiencing a high volume of frustration and suicidal ideation, please continue to hold.

Press 7 if your attention is indivisible.

Press 8 to swallow your own question like an Oroborus.

There are 50 callers ahead of you, with questions poised to march from their mouths like lemmings.

Press 9 if you sense the squared space of this instant.

Know that we value your time spent battling the controlled bureaucracy of your own futility in these moments of discontent.

Press 11 to reach the administration of misunderstandings and alienation.

If you have fashioned the phone cord into a ligature
wide enough for your neck, please hang up and dial 911.

Press 33 if you are feeling mysteriously Masonic
or particularly prophetic.

Know, at this moment, one million ears
press insistent on cold receivers.

Thirteenth Floor

I sweep my hand down
across the string section
of telephone wires.
A few bird notes fly out
as a dusk tone settles
the city beneath me.
Lit and drunk on a roof top
of a twelve-story building
that is not my own,
the slice of city
below is an orchestra pit
I might fall into.
Imagine that sound —
each building's face an industrial
grand piano, tilted sideways —
the alternating dark and florescent
windows are keys I might slide across,
skin staccato against their cold
metal frames. I'm so high,
and high up, leaning over
the brick edge, I could melt
into the street music.
Toy horn section of tiny cars,
cymbal crash of construction metal,
an oboe pitch of moon clears its throat
through the blushing saxophone sky.
The clouds, a purple treble,
puffed out copper edges.
Twilight deepens—a baritone drone bagpipe
flannel falling in measured tartan tones.
I long to scale the octaves,
so high but pulled to float low,

conduct this urban symphony
in flight, tuning fork bones vibrate
as the bell of my beer bottle rings
against the roof's rim.
I stretch my torso over the edge
of the pit, want to lose all my selves,
break the fourth wall, open my lips
to the mouthpiece, throat hungry
for reed, and stroke my spine
across the gathering violin-bowed
strain of night.
If my legs slide over
I could hold the wood,
strum fingers against
the nylon gut between staccato stars,
tend the glass harp, angel organ,
dive into this seraphim sea
through the crescendo
nearly over the edge.

III

Rosemary, that's for Remembrance...

"We misfits are the ones with the ability to enter grief. Death. Trauma. And emerge."

~Lidia Yuknavitch, *The Misfit's Manifesto*

The Archivists

for DLT

It was decreed as we slept,
before smokestacks
bloomed and oil seeped
into our veins congealing
superstition into currency,
the dead must be forgiven.

The living must gather
lined along pews, kneeling
onto unyielding wood to testify.
Hymns, empty exalted verses,
the last rites that confess
the wrongs out the chapel—
flying up bleeding battered
winged rats— yet every swiveled face
swears it saw doves: each a
tender, white-breasted page
that all the clotted memories
fall from like ashes
to the crematorium floor.

Then there are hands that clutch
the Etch-a-Sketch board of memory
and grow small—too honestly small
to shake clean the screen's imprinted
damask layer upon layer. These hearts
refuse to believe that what we forget
is more important than what is remembered.
Recognize forgiveness is not a story's final
punctuation but an empty altar unworthy

of devotion: the bent knee, the bowed head,
the fist in the chest pressed flat
by griddle-iron need
to be okay, to be okay, to be at peace.

Yet, the ones who bow heads,
sutured to their history,
pull away. They can't untie
the ending they desire from the one
the years weave, threads trailing
off the edge like ellipses off a page
through the silence, the cavernous
pause balanced before them.
They only see their own hands
pressed together, refusing all
the emptiness in each palm—
all that was unspoken distilled
to the clean line of epitaph.
Believing what is written on stone
more lasting than what is transcribed
into flesh. They only see a hole
in the ground that must be filled
with something.

Daybook of the Dead

>with a line by Donald Justice

The dead don't
get around much anymore.
Door-stop coffins,
button eyes,
no chores—
maybe some easy gardening.
Useful in their rigor mortis
repose, maybe mannequins,
if you can stand the smell.
Taxidermy scarecrows,
androgynous monotone
dreams.
If you listen silently for
seven months you may
begin to decipher the didactic
sermons that sent them off.
Each popped like a pea out the sheath
of their leaf on the family tree.
Even postmortem
they grow and they grow
in the years populated
by the blood they left
or the skin they touched.
Bloated like drowning
victims, regardless of
how last breaths
were spent,
until they cannot hold
the soaked weight of their own
memory any longer.
Then like a vacant overgrown

lot, they deflate—
once again flat and vegetative—
uncoiled DNA.
Still, holidays are
less stressful
for the dead.
Their daybooks linger
open in the middle of
an empty table:
to-do lists short
as winter days
and no use for
day coats.

Time

Time is an old man with Alzheimer's.
History hinges where wrinkled wrist
meets gnarl of wood cane.
Fate and Destiny hum brightly, dispersing air
into birds named Promise and Presumption.
The gauze lady at Time's side is Luck.
She sweeps an arm, this one lithe and pale,
a moonbeam slicing through wooden boards,
a rotting shed, even the succulents wither.
Breath slides flat on the floor
beside the heart, still as laundry.
Her other arm ascends; round, fleshed, and ruddy.
Skies split open, constellations bloom, spill like laughter
echoing between Possibility and Circumstance—
the tuning forks of Chance twining melodious decay.
And it is always always midnight here
and Time becomes an old man in constant forgetting
and Luck is always the lady reminding,
sometimes through velvet smile,
sometimes through clenched-tooth whispers,
changing the story,
the story always changing.

I Find You

A Love poem for my favorite hedonist accomplice
in Crime, JQB

Living in unraveling time,
I waste with you.
In time beyond facts,
perhaps cigarettes
have given up their poison.
In bodies that remind us
we are dying,
we take our hedonism seriously.
Living in the broken clock
our limbs are minutes.
In the space of time our nails
curl into seconds.
In the seconds we share
between ice cubes melting,
we condensate on tumblers.
We tumble through time
in the late of news stories breaking.
The fragments of story press mosaics
across our broken backs.
We peel the impression left
on sheets across the morning.

Twenty Year Age Difference

We only notice it when
someone is dying. Or dies.
And lately we go to memorials
like Greeks go to christenings.

When my chronic illness
takes us to doctors' offices or hospitals,
which we attend like friends do
clubs and concert venues.

We did vow to push the wheelchair
of whoever was struck lame
and drooling first.
It was me, the younger;
I'm impatient like that.

Sometimes in the edges
of a birthday candle
at a big celebration
or a lit cigarette,
both of which we vow to give up
with increasing regularity.

In lawyers' offices,
tying up the loose ends of my dead,
and, believe me, they can leave
hydras in their wake.

Sometimes, when a psychedelic light
glows fifteen years into the future.
And he is my Burroughs in flesh:
"most natural painkiller what there is."

We are two beings
never much concerned
by their own ends.

Yet, now, when our eyes meet,
the reflection of a bowed cloaked head,
sickle raised, frames the edges—
like depictions above
that bridge in Switzerland.

It flickers briefly, a silent
almost imperceptible nod,
until the stubborn shadow passes.

Then, blue meets greenish hazel.
And, what will be dims
in flashes of who we have been
and are becoming.

Every to-do list's
unwritten italics
remind us to make
each *hello* last
against a horizon of
gathering *goodbyes.*

Biography

My mother is a hospital bed.

My mother is a glamorous 5'10
in her long cut slacks.

My mother is steel and metal plowing cold linoleum.

My mother is a hand model at 16 in New York.

My mother is a POW inside her skin.

My mother is a textbook editor in her 30s.

My mother is hemorrhaging morphine metaphors at the mouth.

My mother is a crossword Sudoku queen.

My mother swears she's been probed by aliens;
they watch us now, and wait.

My mother is all perfumed in her cigarette plumes, anointed
in sweet white wine and lit by a Hawaiian sunset.

My mother hisses at the well-dressed palliative care doctor
every time she walks in her room.

My mother calls her the Angel of Death.

My mother whispers to me and giggles about toe-faeries
as i massage her feet.

My mother is a Japanese wood cutting.

My mother's voice is not my mother's voice.

My mother was called communist by a smalltown cop because she wore black and read Beat poetry.

My mother is all X-rays and radioactive dyes.

My mother loses her love: impaled on a trap in Vietnam.

My mother contains a PICC line to another dimension.

My mother marries her high school boyfriend to move to London.

My mother is shrinking like dry sands in high tide.

My mother sees her aunt in flames on a movie screen the day a lit cigarette eats the bed.

My mother dreams the death of another in an early morning news radio headline.

My mother marries her divorce attorney.

My mother is the recoil left behind a fired gun.

My mother adopts all my friends and lovers while i orphan myself for years.

My mother and i recognize each other the night her arm grows four times its size.

My mother nearly drowns as a child.

My mother sees her body underwater from a tree branch above.

My mother reads Runes to us every New Years Day.

My mother is an octopus, her translucent tentacles all inked out.

My mother wears falls, dresses like Twiggy, looks like
a young Catherine Denueve.

My mother is a pharaoh, tugging the tubes in her sarcophagus,
wild-eyed, summoning us all to follow.

Life Lines

How they cross each other,
find each other, leave each other,
intersect and diverge.

Who will go, and
how far can we travel
through the stinging wind
and dunes of nothing,
everything at stake?

How far will
our voices carry?

What harmonies will grow,
and how do we sing
with our throats on
fire and our skins burning?

These skins are our songs.
Let's put our ears
to every pore and use
the pain for kindling.

The Release

after my late friend Heather Anne Welch's painting, The Release

There's a euphoria
that settles over
the room of the dead
after a long dying.
Potent as poison,
though you can't seek it out.
Infused with the blur
of vivid deliriums—
no sleep and less rest—
you must tune into it.
Like the language of leaves,
you can channel its frequency,
ride on the waves
which give you strength—
widening like an
unexpected smile,
like arms growing
round enough to hold others.
There's an ecstasy,
that spreads like wings,
which carry the Self
clean over the eaves.
There's a map of Self
receding behind you.
A vortex of wind
billowing what's left
through that last harrowing mile.
Until you are molecules,
a confetti finale,
a star system expanding,

a soft chill in a quiet room.
There's a portal
in the hollow of bones
where the marrow burns
dizzy, geometric, electric.
Constructs are torn
like carrion by vultures,
those ravenous morticians
tearing meat from ribs
that cage the heart
that pumps the blood
when creatures are carnal.
There's elation in the Self receding.
The backlit impermanence
of this created world
where planets implode
and each social system's weight
turns to ash on the pyre.
You can't seek it out.
You must stay and bear witness,
tune its frequency.
Explore the underworld
with an agency
Persephone was not often
attributed in tales.
There's release at the end of this portal,
though pain to pass through,
a secret buried in space.
The secret is a whisper:
we are blind to the vortexes
surrounding us daily,
or we sense them and turn away.
Next time you see one, bend into it;
hold the hands of your dead.

When you can breathe
to ten, step through.
You may follow your dead
in their exaltation
past our nightmares, which are portals.
To that *only way out is through*.
We can create what we need
to survive if we follow the waves.
The impossible is pain.
Yet, pain is a portal—
rapture on the other side.
You can see it without
and then through,
once it's in you.
It's like the dark stars
in the city skies.
The ones you can't see
but you know are there.

Half the Story

for HAW:

*you have given me the gift of permission
and the assurance
that the process of surrender
for both chronic and terminal can be a creative endeavor.
I will follow you as far as language and skin allow...*

Today, tonight,
my stomach sounds like yours
again.
But mine is an air raid siren,
while yours counts down days
to Hiroshima.

Today, tonight,
I ride a boat on tsunami seas,
yet I see land
strokes away.
It is balmy and golden there.

It does not matter.
You cannot feel it.
You can't be
where you can't feel
what surrounds you.

Today, tonight,
as your tiny boat shrinks untethered,
I see you skirting my stormy bay
out into open water.
I want to yell out, while we still
have ears to hear, and
the life vest of logic inflates
just above the raging tide:
In this life we've been enough.

You once ably captained
your sound vessel through
the seaweed and brine.
Now she funnels the sea through
her holes, and mine grows
corroded by life, even as
the mast does not tip.
Yet every breath uncorks new casks
of toxin, and nausea replaces
the salt in the air.

We are at a picnic
instead of a funeral,
for once, again.

Feel the soft sand
of the shore
under our toes,
interlock fingers,
and run...

Do You

Remember
(burnout velvet scarf slid over shoulder blade)
how
(rubber heel tips echoed on cement)
I
(muffled laughter, stale gin, lighter fluid)
used
(discarded, spent, crumpled on the floor)
to dance?
(questions whispered in the ear after midnight)

Coffee Grounds

In the ICU,
ammonia amnesia
eviscerates the familiar
from memory's mechanisms.
Machines dictate heartbeats,
each pressed breath
a countdown.
Tubes are crossing guards
ushering fluids in
and toxins out.
Gauze tape flags
direct the sway
between self and ether.
The beat between
the in and out
grows longer,
as self compresses
into other.
Whirring and bubbling
eat at the linear
measure of time
until the beeping
swallows the senses
in the clean back kitchen
of the soul:
clanging anonymously
behind the warm revelry
of a full banquet hall.
The symphony of being
recedes into specific jobs,
clean of their relational interdependence.
Remembrance slides antiseptic

off the mop, the spray, the corridors
buzzing fluorescent.
Yet in each sterile cell,
the body insists.
Its wastes flush and bubble
even as the veins retreat.
Even in this antiseptic cathedral
with clean confessionals and
chemical communions
the smell of rotting
resists erasure.
In the end, it's the shock
of coffee grounds
that deafens the death scent:
two hands setting out
cups of unlikely dirt.
Used filters
held before pastel smocks—
elemental and earthly—
placed on nurses' desks
next to buzzing phones,
in the stock closets
full of vacuum-sealed silver needles,
and the side tables of each room.
These offerings, these votives,
like forgotten marrow,
something for memory to sieve through.

Smiles of my Dead

Lately, I find myself wearing
the smiles of my dead.

My laughter floats atop theirs
like small weights on weather balloons.

Someone in a room or in the phone
shares something.
And another, who is absent,
takes over my expression.

Cat's crinkled nose,
her pursed lips wrinkling
'round piercings,
nostrils slightly flared.

Mom's throaty staccato notes,
a tune we shared at times.
One I coveted on days
she secreted it away
for her less intimate public.

The warm
melting Heather's
constant cool.
When her smile broke,
the temperature rose
around her.

Dad's nearly silent chesty rasp
rippling out, head back,
impish eyes sparkling.

The laugh scored when I
one up'd him with a terrible joke,
or pretended to bristle
at one of his own.

This alchemy is no death mask.
They are teaching me how to smile again.

The Humans

had a strange run.
They always thought
they were talking to each other.

They licked their fingers to paper
and folded up their hearts,
but stuffed them into sock drawers.

Paper cut deeper
than daggers
until the keyboard—

the tap-tap of resonant notes,
of dissonant notes.
They used them to strike,

but could not hear the music.
They signed their souls to Truth,
but seldom knew honesty.

Desperate to be heard,
they forgot
how to listen.

Now every window
lights an author,
audience dissolving.

Obsessed with finding
themselves,
each hallway grew mirrors.

All they desired
was there in the reflection
of Other.

As ages passed, they created
experts for finding what they lost,
but forgot how to see.

Sometimes, though,
they saw each other
just before leaving.

What We're Left with Sometimes

Her last words
His last look
Last hospital visit
Clay paw prints
Worn gas mask
Rented death bed
Singed lace bra
Cobalt bobbed wig
Unsent birthday card
Stuffed trash bags
for Goodwill
Chipped nesting doll
Reverse mortgage
Adult diapers
Old photographs
of unknown faces
Blue morphine
Self-help books
Broken lava lamp
Private journal confession
Long probates
One thousand last cigarettes
and one very last December

Chronic vs Terminal

either way, so many sad [i]
bouquets [ii] you'll never see.

perhaps the difference is [iii] life
in prison" versus the death [iv] sentence –
waterboarded for life or being [v]
burned alive.[vi]

either way, the body [vii] has more
ways to say, "no" than there are
languages on Earth."""

the hunger [viii] always comes back#
when the pain## subsides.
have you ever counted all the ~~ways~~ (styles, directions, trajectories)
(in which) desire takes flight? [ix]

the only way out is through the skin@

Martyrs%% are ~~poignant~~ but
useless. [x]

~~the blood and the brain cells die~~&
~~organs give~~&&
~~bones degrade~~&&&

the Zen monk was wrong. [xi]
even angels trade [xii]
their solemn eternities [xiii]
for a chance at one-hundred last suppers. [xiv]

[i] See throat, pen, butcher's knife
[ii] the pace at which an orchid is pared[*]
[iii] to be...
[iv] the Tequila worm, the Green Faerie, an anis Ouzo's tannin flood of perennial fennel seeds, yellow petals spreading over thirsty continents
[v] or nothingness
[vi] and "There is nothing to fear[***]but fear itself[****]
[vii] each hair on the skin can scream louder than the ear can register[$]
[viii] and still, even my hungers have hungers[$$]:
[ix] Marion on the trapeze[###]
[x] the angel standing stoic beneath her,
in the shadow of her swinging flesh
wishing to want, yearning to feel[%]
[xi] he grows more terminal each day
[xii] each sense ignites
[xiii] then dusks out
[xiv] like fireflies, dying, midsummer, too soon

[*] sliced to naked nape
[**] see Frida Kahlo's *Broken Column*
[***] see Red Scare, see Great Satan, see Oblivion
[****] remember that time you were retching or after surgery how the whole world

evaporated. (As illustrated, we survive only because we can forget specificity)
[*****] see deaf person stabbed, see pit bull strapped in rape stand, see blue baby
[$] see dog whistle, see broken deer caller, see Diamanda Gallas, see Yma Sumac
[$$] see "weird abundance" (Sexton, "The Black Art")
[#] "thought we said goodbye last night" (Holiday's "Goodmorning Heartache")
[##] "here you are with the dawn" (ditto)
[###] "... goodmorning heartache, sit down ..." (ditto goddammit)
[%] strange fruit hanging, burning flesh
[%%] see Persephone, see Joan of Arc, see Jesus, see Sharon Tate
[@] see Chinese Torture (Bataille, *Tears of Eros* 204)
[&] see poppy paper, see sticky notes
[&&] see power outage
[&&&] see trembling cane, see blank stare, see miracle, see tombstone

CODA:

Reflections

Untitled #1

by Heather Anne Welch (2013)

my body is a two-way street
my body is a hit parade
my body is a problem child
my body is a thousand times
my body is a box car died
my body is a ticket taker
my body is a way to get there
my body is a tuning fork
my body is the west in winter
my body is a place to crash.

I don't take any forms of Payment

Untitled #2

By Jennifer Bradpiece (2019)

my body is a strangled vine
my body is a pin cushion
my body is a chemistry set
my body is a Jag on blocks
my body is a lab rat fried
my body is a tourniquet
my body is a delinquent house guest
my body is a skipping record
my body is a weathervane
my body is Kahlo's *Broken Column*.

I don't remember how to stay Here

I would like to express deep gratitude for the following humans and entities without which this project and my current writing life would be far less possible and pleasurable: David Tripp Thee Magic Worm, Pondwater Society (especially my Joanne Qualey Baines & King Daddy), Cat Angelique McIntire, Heather Anne Welch, The Badass Boob Poets, Arminé Iknadossian, Betsy Kenoff-Boyd, Brendan Constantine, Peggy Dobreer, The Ugly Mug, Nyx the Cat, Coffee Cartel, Whisky & Poetry Salon, and my Lemur support creature for seeing me through the pain always.

And finally, I extend my thanks to Jeff Alfier & Tobi Alfier of Blue Horse Press for lovingly publishing this book and all the beautiful ways they show up in our community.

About the Author

Photo credit: Giuliana Maresca

Jennifer Bradpiece was born and raised in the multifaceted muse, Los Angeles, where she still resides. She has interned at Beyond Baroque and remains active in the L.A. writing and art scene. Project collaborations with multi-media artists, far and near, feed her passion. Jennifer's poetry has been nominated for a Pushcart Prize and published in various anthologies, journals, and online zines, including *Redactions*, *The Common Ground Review,* and *The Bacopa Literary Review*. She is the author of *Lullabies for End Times* (Moon Tide Press, 2020).

www.ingramcontent.com/pod-product-compliance
Lightning Source LLC
LaVergne TN
LVHW041301080426
835510LV00009B/833